Lots of
love
x Mummy x
x x

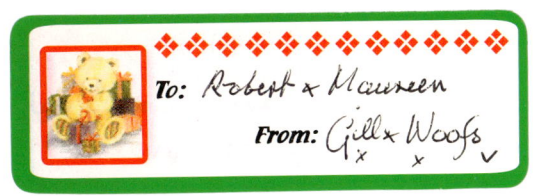

ALL OUR DAYS

Edited by

Heather Killingray

First published in Great Britain in 2002 by
ANCHOR BOOKS
Remus House,
Coltsfoot Drive,
Peterborough, PE2 9JX
Telephone (01733) 898102

All Rights Reserved

Copyright Contributors 2002

HB ISBN 1 84418 048 4
SB ISBN 1 84418 049 2

Foreword

Anchor Books is a small press, established in 1992, with the aim of promoting readable poetry to as wide an audience as possible.

We hope to establish an outlet for writers of poetry who may have struggled to see their work in print.

The poems presented here have been selected from many entries and as always editing proved to be a difficult task.

I trust this selection will delight and please the authors and all those who enjoy reading poetry.

Heather Killingray
Editor

CONTENTS

The Creek And Yachts	Rosemary E Pearson	1
Nostalgic View	C Tyler	2
Spider Alert	Sally Wyatt	3
Leaving	L Gill	4
Afraid	Vivienne Anne Thomson	5
Boredom	Joy Bartelt	6
Forever Friends	J Craven	7
A World That Still Knows Love	Kathleen Why	8
Bishop Street	Angela Moore	9
Sexy Louise	Barry Ryan	10
Time	Edward Elwell	11
Dreams	S S Jackson	12
So Pleased To Meet You	Cheremane Hartery	13
Golden Days Of Summer	Marjorie Leyshon	14
Grand-Daughters	R Sackley	15
The Alternative	Gertrude M Black	16
Hard Up	Graham Robertson	17
The Smile	Angela R Davies	18
Pennine Gale	Terence Leslie	19
The Spider	Rosmary Healy	20
The Best Things In Life Are Free	Peter J Sutton	21
People Watching	Heather R E Cox	22
Aye Toddlin On	L Niven	23
I Had A Dream	Debra Dawson	24
To The Beach	Dave Deakin	25
My Pussy	Peggy C	26
The Newsreader	Duncan Cook	27
Sormy Nightmare!	Marjorie Cowan	28
Muttley Calling - Where's Me Medal?	John Smurthwaite	29
Through Fear To Hope	Wilhelmina Cobb	30
Night-Time Noises	Gemma Gibbs	31
Fingers And Toes	Jim Pritchard	32
Parsley	Eve Kimber	33
Linger Longer!	Tricia Layton	34
Moods	Molly Phasey	35

Title	Author	Page
Pisces	E M Eagle	36
Brockhill Park - Hysterics In The Hail	Carey Sellwood	37
The Three Ghostly Miners	P Bradley	38
Couldn't Care Less	Matthew L Burns	39
Sand Martins	Barry G Randall	40
The Dull Life	Len Corner	41
Most Of All	Jeffrey Kelly	42
Spread A Little Sunshine	Vera Ewers	43
On Coloured Wings	Joan Smith	44
Down On The Farm	Maggy Copeland	46
I Do It To Music Occasionally	Owen Watson	47
Report Card	Andrew Younger	48
Journey Afloat	Sharon Christian	49
Magic Spot	S J Dodwell	50
End In Sight	C M Creedon	51
Walking In The Dark	Joan Chapman	52
A Cry From The Heart	Jacqueline Bartlett	53
Whispers	J Mstoles	54
Yes, It's Good	Stella Bush-Payne	55
Auntie Ethel's Ghost	Andrew Detheridge	56
Hastings	John Wayre	58
Life Near The Stream	Edith Buckeridge	59
Whispering Shadows	D J Abbott	60
Day Trips	Tom Usher	61
DIY	George S Johnstone	62
Wishing You Safe	Julie Brown	64
The Poor Potato	Violetta Jean Ferguson	65
No Quiet Place	Brian Norman	66
Findon	G Carpenter	67
A Case Of Conflict	Geoffrey Wilyman	68
The Wave	S Woodland	69
Galloping On The Moor	C Armstrong	70
Life's Story	R Baker	71
The Dentist	Christine M Wicks	72
Motcombe Park	Tim Sharman	73
Tears	S M Ilsley	74
Watch The TV	Keith L Powell	75

Poetry	B Spinks	76
Faces In The Crowd	Jean Bradbury	77
Summer Camp In America	S M Robertson	78
The Paintbrush	Rosemary Smith	79
Ah Vanity	Alistair McLean	80
Modern Times	Patricia McQueen	81
Rise And Shine	Alan Johnson	82
Here Comes The Sun	Jessie Coffey	83
Time	Kay Taylor	84
Call Of Devon	Margaret Gurney	86
Waiting For You	M Marshall	87
False April	Pat Saunders	88
Jubilee	Mary Crowhurst	89
Untitled	Arthur J Pullen	90
Eating Companion	Joanne Wilcock	91
The Washing	C Matthews	92
New Found Confidence	Doreen Kowalska	93
The Shadow	D Field	94
Wishful Thinking	Hetty Foster	95
The Bean Shaped Tree	Jean Bald	96

THE CREEK AND YACHTS
(Noss Mayo)

They lie there eloquently
Like ghosts in the autumn haze,
Lying at anchor beneath the squall,
They watch, as young children play.

Silently they yawn majestically there,
As we watch the swans dabbling,
Fishing under the water for minnows,
I could but only wonder, stop and stare.

The still water laps at the bows,
Tilting there, from start to stern,
The tide retreating, as we continue to stare
At the mystical world we care to share.

The air cool, but warm in breath,
We watch the water breathe in and out,
As the sleepy village towers above the slopes,
Watching silently, with tender view.

Now we return to the warmth of a fire,
As we turn our way onwards, back to home,
Leaving this scene, softly given,
By a strange light, we travel forth.

Rosemary E Pearson

NOSTALGIC VIEW

I wish that mornings were the same,
The swirl of mist, that hint of rain?
The cuckoo's faint but haunting cry.
A hint of pink in dawning sky.
And swallows soaring high - so high,
A world at peace

I think of swans among the reeds,
A glint of water in the trees -
I see the fields, the young green corn,
A pheasant struts across the lawn,
And rabbits, playing in the dawn
Are silent, in the peace

The daily flight of honking geese,
My heart can sing with sounds like these -
In early light - that eerie call?
O'er lake and river, house and hall,
And their return as evening falls
Does not offend the peace

The swans remain, the river too -
But now a road impedes my view,
The dust is red, the banks are high,
A roar of traffic fills the sky -
Few birds remain, to sing - or fly
For where is now the peace?

C Tyler

SPIDER ALERT
(Dedicated to Auntie Eileen Lee)

Incy Wincy spider . . . climbed up the spout
Down came the rain . . . and washed the spider out . . .

So much for the spider . . . never tiring
His cobweb full of diamonds . . . nature inspiring.

So unassuming in their being
All those eyes . . . there for the seeing

Hopping from twig to twig
This miraculous safety net begin to knit . . .

Did you really frighten away Miss Muffet
I don't actually give a tuffet . . .

Some with legs spindly . . . some very hairy
Washed down the sink . . . cos they look scary . . .

I try to understand why so few people like you
Is it your attitude or *wot*?

Oh I am so sorry I pushed you out of any orrifice
That I so conveniently found . . . and sent you tumbling to the ground
Called you all the B's and F's . . . and made an ear shattering
Screeching sound . . .

So spider . . . spider . . . I didn't mean to kill you
Forgive me I was ignorant . . . believe me will you . . .

Out came the sunshine . . . and dried up all the rain
So Incy Wincy spider . . . climbed the spout again . . .

Sally Wyatt

LEAVING

I hate the way you have to leave,
to see you walk away.
I need you with me, to hold me close.
I wish that you could stay.

I love the way you make me smile,
without a single word.
The way you seem to sing a song,
that I have never heard.

I miss the way you look at me,
the sparkle in your eye.
I love the way I trust you so
I know you'd never lie.

But most of all, the thing I need,
the thing I miss and want and most of all,
the thing I love just has to be . . . you.

L Gill

AFRAID

Life is hard to face when one has an illness,
When time is rushing fast and you wonder what to do next,
Is there such a thing as fulfilment?
When all one does is to get vexed.

One has to think whether to get help or not,
Wondering what tomorrow has in store,
Your brain works too hard, it gets so hot,
When you depend on your last hopes you lie helplessly on the floor,

Is this illness in your mind or is it real?
You want help but you are afraid to seek it,
Are you wondering where to get your next meal?
This is not a game, you are in the pit.

Vivienne Anne Thomson

BOREDOM

Sitting alone, counting the minutes.
Feeling the pulse for a sign of life!
Tick tocking the hours.
Lazing away the days.
Sipping a drink trying to make it last longer
Eating away at life into the stomach.
What oh what a way to exist.
When will life become life
not a memory?
Where has speech gone?
Where has talk gone?
Everything seems so long, long, long
Bedtime is never-ending.
Into the night, into the dawn.
What can be at the end of it?
Surely something better?
Probably, probably it's reality,
trying to get a grip on something.
Shame! Shame!

Joy Bartelt

FOREVER FRIENDS

Forgive and forget, and never fret,
Helps you along life's way.
There's many heartaches within this world,
We encounter day by day.
People who have learnt to share,
Have their troubles halved by those who care.
Friendship is a blessing, to all who understand.

With a faithful friend who's always there ready to lend a hand.
You hold your trust in those you love, and stand together side by side,
Through the darkness we never forget, although we never can see
What lies before, the way ahead, or how things are meant to be.
A guiding hand awaits you and leads you along life's way,
Then the light that shines upon you, turns your darkness into day.

J Craven

A World That Still Knows Love

Life is just a journey
We may travel for a span,
So let us make the most of it
And do the best we can.

Understanding may not come easy
While our world's in such a plight
But it's up to us just to carry on
And to do what we think right.

Ignoring all the jealousy
The hatred and the greed
It's hard God knows without His help
To try to recognise man's needs.

With all the growing discontent
That burns within man's soul,
No wonder we get down at times
And lose sight of our goal.

But if we pray within ourselves
Seeking courage from above,
I'm sure that God will help us find
A world that still knows love . . .

Kathleen Why

BISHOP STREET

Lovely Bishop Street, glorious, historic and very old
A place where many stories and legends would unfold
Both within and without the Walls, I am told
Some tales were warm-hearted and romantic, others
                              sad, tragic and cold.

Throughout the street, there are famous fine buildings galore,
The Courthouse, Bishop's Palace, Lumen Christi College and more
My grandparents' house with its polished door proudly stood here
This was a home bursting with love, warmth and welcoming cheer.

Many happy childhood days, I spent with my family there
Dear relatives and friends were so kind and full of care
These very special people stay evergreen on my mind
The old street was the best you could ever find.

I remember the Stone outside Charlotte and Sarah's door
There I would rest, then skip and play some more
Wee Rose by the lamp post, would always send me to the shop
She needed supplies, from the little store beside the bus stop.

Like the rest of the world, Bishop Street has changed quite a lot
But still there, are the treasured, important values of life I got
The hands of time move on relentless and quickly for us all
Yet this great majestic street reigns sublime and timeless over all.

Angela Moore

SEXY LOUISE

Louise is a very sexy lady I met,
adult, slim, and brunette!
She is kind, caring and considerate,
living in London, this place is her favourite.

She wants to be a 'Nicky Clarke' successor,
and be a great hairdresser!
Having her own saloon, for public and stars,
afterwards, meeting them all in the bars!

I really like to see her again,
at her 'Foster Mum's' den!
But we have to wait and see,
if she really likes me!
But at last this poem is nearly at an end,
unfortunately for me, she has a boyfriend!

Barry Ryan

TIME

What is time? What is it all about?
It's the strangest of things, of that there's no doubt.
For time, does not come through a wire,
You may have it to kill, but it won't expire.
It doesn't come through pipes like gas,
And we have no choice, but to let it pass.

Where it comes from, or where it goes, we cannot tell.
For it cannot be seen, and it has no smell.
But the thing, I cannot understand,
Is though you can have time on your hands,
It's something that you cannot feel,
Yet somehow, it has the power to heal.

Edward Elwell

DREAMS

In my dreams, I've travelled far,
around the world, by my wings,
not my car.
I've been over valleys and deep blue seas,
across a desert, on a calming breeze.
I feel the wind, with its magic embrace,
blowing cool air, upon my feathered face.
I've been to the planets, the sun and the moon,
problem is, I'm back too soon.
In my dreams, I couldn't see,
the vision of a cruel reality.
Within my dreams, I am free,
to release the spirit, in the heart of me.

S S Jackson

SO PLEASED TO MEET YOU

You were born at 7.32
And *boy* were we glad to see you
Nine whole months in Mummy's tummy
I hope you were pleased to see us too

You had ten little fingers
And ten little toes
Lots of dark brown hair
Then you opened your eyes and gave me a stare

Mummy cuddled you
And then Daddy too
And finally I got to meet you
Which I couldn't wait to do

I held you in my arms
And thought straight away you were so full of charm
You were so neat
But far from petite

I fed you your first bottle
Which you drank like a doddle
Then I dressed you up neat
And then put you to sleep

By the way I'm Cheremane
I'm so pleased to meet you
And Daniel you can call me 'Mane'

Cheremane Hartery

GOLDEN DAYS OF SUMMER

On golden days of summer when skies are blue, the sun is high
It is blissful just to laze around and look up to the sky
Sometimes a lonely puff of cloud will drift across your scene
You wonder where it's going and also where it's been.
A skylark wings its merry way soaring whilst singing its song
A blackbird joins with sounds so sweet to help the trills along
The bees are very busy as they toil from flower to flower
Their drone so soporific as we while away an hour
Enjoying the warmth of sunshine a doze would be so right
So happy doing nothing, your thoughts just seem so light
Away they go so lazily think of nothing to break the calm
A golden day of summer to everyone a balm
To watch the clouds, to hear the birds, to see leaves dancing in a breeze,
What solace and what joy it brings to be so much at ease
To lie there so contented - the time goes passing by
No need to fuss or bother nor really question why
Take pleasure from the moment the radiance of the sun
The colours of the garden, the sounds of summer fun.

Marjorie Leyshon

GRANDDAUGHTERS

Grammie, dear Grammie,
please come for a walk,
tell me those stories while you talk,
'Who lives in this house?'
'A man with a mouse.'
'Who lives in this house?'
'A gran with a goat.'
Grammie what wonderful stories
you have to tell,
of faces and places you have in your mind.

On the way home my friend did appear,
o'dear, o'dear,
'May I walk with you, on your way home?'
'Go away,' said a small voice.
'Go away do you hear?'
'We don't want you with us,'
came a voice from the chair.

What could I say?
My friend understood, and went on her way.
She has grandchildren too,
I am pleased to say
Then we went home and had tea with the fairies.

R Sackley

THE ALTERNATIVE

It is quite hard, this getting old
My neck is sore, my feet are cold,
And when I hear my knee bones creak
I'm feeling like a human freak.

My eyes grow dim and slow my walk
I start to stammer when I talk.
I used to hear 'the green grass grow'
Alas! This is no longer so.

My memory used to be fantastic
But is no longer so elastic
Events that did not worry me
Seem like a nightmare now to be.

At night in bed to flee the pain
I toss and look for sleep in vain
And when I wake, start getting busy
I stumble for my head gets dizzy.

As life was really not much fun
I thought, I'll ask my doctor son:
When smiling kindly I was told:
'There is *one* way: *not* getting old.'

Gertrude M Black

HARD UP

A shopping you went, all your money you spent, he joked not a thing did you buy your old dad.
An old penny chew or a sweety or two, to stop him from feeling so sad
Growing up was so tough and he had it quite tough, you could say that he didn't have much.
His sister's old jeans that he wore till his teens, and a rabbit that lived in a hutch.

He had but few joys, just a few Dinky toys, bought with coppers he'd saved for a treat.
Shopping for fags or the odd Wonderloaf for the lady that lived down the street.
In his little old home with no bath and no phone, just one fire to generate heat,
He lived with his mum and two sisters as well, they struggled to make ends meet.

Bringing up three, well it must have been tough, no Social to help his mum cope.
Just scrubbing the floors in the old Co-op shop, a dream win on the Pools, not a hope.
No luxuries did he crave, he just had to save, for pocket money he never had as a kid.
When his shoes they wore out from kicking a football about, he stuffed them with card, well they all did!

But time it moves on, and those hard times have gone, double glazing, central heating he's now got.
But is life any better? He supposes it must be. Would he want to go back? I think not.
So just bear in mind about a dad who's so kind, he wants you to have more than he.
He's got it all now, he's got you and your mum, and that's as rich as any man could be.

Graham Robertson

THE SMILE

A man smiled at me today,
not in any sexual way
you understand,
but more a mental profering of hand,
a silent recognition of my worth,
a mutual, common purpose on this Earth.

A woman smiled at me today,
somewhat grudgingly, as if to say
are you friend or foe -
even a threat? I need to know
before I permit a glimpse of soul,
acknowledging a mutual goal.

A child smiled at me today
in a trusting and disarming way,
expecting nothing, giving all,
accepting me without recall.
Not a single word was spoken,
a soothing silence lay unbroken.

And is a smile so very rare
because we fear this laying bare,
exposure of our faults and flaws
opening up those long-closed doors?
And are there lessons to be learned,
is true respect hard-won or earned?

Angela R Davies

PENNINE GALE

Roar loud chill Pennine breeze
rustle cotton grass and trees
howl hard against the grey stone walls
of farms and cottages, mills and halls

Blow forth the wheeling curlew's cry
from bleak and misty moorland high
gather the rain clouds thick and black
cast deluge down on mountain track

Where streams of rushing water pour
from peaty bog to valley floor
and there as rivers wide and deep
flow on past fields of grazing sheep

And with your breath like driven snow
tell stories of days long ago
of weary working man and wife
who trod the cobbled streets of life

Back and forth from home to mill
their humble duty to fulfil
to work in atmosphere so dull
slaves to the chains of cotton and wool.

Terence Leslie

THE SPIDER

A spider spreads its web
Like a silkworm in a mulberry tree
The web shines in morning dew
Raindrops fall like diamonds on a ring
It's so beautiful yet so deadly
It's for the spider to catch its prey
If a fly lands, it's his last day
The spider jumps like a lion to a man
Eating flesh as quick as she can
Or if her hunger has just then passed
It spins a web around its prey
To have meat for another day.

Rosmary Healy

THE BEST THINGS IN LIFE ARE FREE

The best things in life are fresh air and sunshine,
The best thing in life, is a song.
For when you are singing, you're happy,
And that helps your life flow along.
The best things are also your friendships,
As well as a healthy lifestyle,
With good friends and good health,
You don't need, too much wealth,
And another good thing, is your smile.
For when you are smiling, you make others smile,
Then the clouds up above, soon roll by.
So smile, and smile often, then those hard thoughts will soften,
And so there'll be no need to cry.
Look for enjoyment, it is useful employment,
Perhaps do someone, a good turn.
It will make you feel better, like receiving a letter
That is something, we all need to learn.
The very best thing in my life, was my own darling wife,
She really was always a treasure.
Wherever I went, whatever I did, to come home to her was a pleasure,
But now she has gone, has long since past on,
And sometimes when I've had a right ear full,
I try to be witty and sing an old ditty,
Then, 'fore long I'm again, feeling cheerful.
So let's have less moaning, and not so much groaning,
As folks, you can take it from me.
Put these best things together, forget the bad weather,
For the best things in life, are still free.

Peter J Sutton

PEOPLE WATCHING

Sitting, watching the people go around
Sounds absurd, yet it's quite profound.
Going about their daily chores
Many colours, shapes and sizes galore.

Sitting, watching the people go around
Maybe a bargain they have found.
Children scolded for their deeds,
When sometimes there is no need.

Sitting, watching the people go around
Some pass by without a sound.
Judging their circumstances as they pass by
Applying criteria that they will satisfy.

Sitting, watching the people go around
A pastime of which I am quite renowned.
The crowds are thinning now - they're on their way
It's drawing towards the end of the day.

Heather R E Cox

AYE TODDLIN ON

(My parents were buried together, they died within hours of one another. They were ages 85 and 87. They died 7th and 8th January 1962. I'll be 87 in 3 months.)

Here I am in 2002
And aye toddlin on!
I can't go out now on my own
So I usually stay at home.

I like to keep myself busy
And never run out of work
I feel I want to show returns
For the time I spend on Earth.

It's a long road looking back
But time and tide has flown
The day is coming soon
When I won't be 'on my own.'

It's been a long road, but happy
Memories loving and sad
Happy home, happy life
And a loving mum and dad.

L Niven

I HAD A DREAM

I had a dream
it lasted one day
I dreamt that my children
had learnt how to play.

I had a dream
that the war had gone
but I knew deep down
it would not last long.

I had a dream
that the planet was saved
and that all of the grown-ups
grew up and behaved.

I had a dream
but like a favourite song
I woke up in the morning
my dream had stopped and gone.

Debra Dawson

TO THE BEACH

I took myself to the beach today,
Seagulls cry and the children play.
And the waves rolled in to sweep away
The castles built in the morning.

I took myself to the beach today,
Sun and sand and a clear calm bay.
And the waves rolled in, in a gentle way
To tickle the toes of the bathers.

I took myself to the beach today,
Wind and rain and a closed café.
And the waves rolled in with thunderous spray
To batter the sea defences.

I took myself to the beach today,
A perfect place for a perfect stay.
And the waves rolled in, in their ceaseless way
To cover the sand completely.

I took myself to the beach today,
A change is as good as a rest, they say.
And the waves rolled out, and without delay
The beach was mine once more.

Dave Deakin

My Pussy

I have a little pussy cat
Who sits and smiles at me
He doesn't miaow or chase around
He just sits and smiles at me

I saw him not so long ago
And his smile attracted me
I thought I'd like him on my desk
Sitting and smiling at me.

He doesn't eat food and he doesn't drink milk
He hasn't a coat that's soft as silk
It's his happy face I love to see
As he just sits and smiles at me.

I really love my little puss
Who sits and smiles at me
Why don't I do aught for him?
He's a china puss, you see!

That doesn't matter one tiny bit
As long as I can see him
Occupying a space on my desk
Sitting and smiling at me.

Peggy C

THE NEWSREADER

I love my job, I read the news,
I tell of gangsters, high on booze.
Of miracle cures and wonder drugs,
And hospitals with superbugs.
Babies abandoned on the street,
And all those stars we'd like to meet.
There's sport of course, with Cheltenham Town,
Could Forest Green be going down?
There's weather too, how will it be,
Sun or rain or quite chilly?
Then in minutes it's all done,
As quickly as it was begun.
Then it's back to desk and chair,
But I'll be back in an hour so don't despair.

Duncan Cook

STORMY NIGHTMARE!

The thunder roared, the lightning flashed
And into the steeple the lightning crashed!
A terrified squawk from the wooden cock -
That petrified me, that was a shock!
Where can I go? What can I do?
'Cock-a-doodle-doodle-doo!'
Suddenly I was small and wee,
And he tucked me under his wing so easily!
He flew with me through the closed church door,
And there was a coffin laid out on the floor!
The cock knocked on the lid with his sharp, fierce beak,
Then suddenly with a piercing creak;
The lid flew open and there a fearsome sight,
Out popped a ghost arrayed in white.
With a look of fury, from his one protruding eye,
'People disturbing me, they surely die!'
Out stretched his arms, like thick branches of oak;
I began to tremble, I began to choke.
Then out of the corner of my eye
A small mouse hole I did espy;
Now in my tiny size I scuttled through;
Back into the fresh air with sky so blue.
I had dozed by a tree, after a picnic of good fare;
And it was there I had had this awful nightmare.

Marjorie Cowan

MUTTLEY CALLING - WHERE'S ME MEDAL?

Another year has come and gone
But still I've no award
I could'a used that fifty quid
On holidays abroad
The judges have decided though
Not in complete accord

Four twisted arms - two broken teeth
Three sport a blackened eye
As editors fought tooth and nail
Both skin and hair did fly
Was it handbags at ten paces?
Believe some snagged their tights
Police were called out several times
To try and break up fights

Was Remus House a shambles
All the furniture wrecked
Was Claire Bull charged with butting
Was Ian Walton decked?
The infighting so vicious
Some remain a cabbage
This mostly the result of
Tangling with Claire Savage

Like Mailer and Hemingway
Both pugnacious writers
Does fighting over prizes
Make them all prizefighters?
For the poets who missed the cut
They may just have blundered
Your poem was lost in those fights
Over the top hundred.

John Smurthwaite

THROUGH FEAR TO HOPE

Fear - Dear - Deal - Dell
Doll - Dole - Dope - Hope

Fear is a feeling we all know in life,
When what we hold *dear* can be lost through strife,
We must learn to *deal* with what is the cause,
Not hide in the *dell*, - attack it with force.
Don't act like a *doll*, all floppy and weak,
Or one on the *dole*, who's future looks bleak,
Don't look for an answer in pills or *dope*,
Be strong, determined and survive through *hope*!

Wilhelmina Cobb

NIGHT-TIME NOISES

The sky begins to darken,
Night is coming near,
The sun no longer guides us,
And shadows will appear.

The streets become so silent,
People disappear,
Noises in my bedroom,
Mum says, 'Goodnight my dear.'

The tree outside the window,
Creates a horrid shape,
I hate the creaking staircase,
I wish I could escape.

A light outside is shining,
Headlights of a car,
I'm starting to get frightened,
Is my bedroom door ajar?

My heart is beating faster,
I try to stay quite calm,
I start to realise,
The shadows mean no harm.

This night will last forever,
I know I'll never sleep,
The solution to my problem,
Might be to count some sheep.

The street no longer silent,
People reappear,
Noises in my bedroom,
Mum calls, 'Wake up my dear!'

__Gemma Gibbs (11)__

FINGERS AND TOES

Aren't toes funny-looking things sticking out on ends of feet,
there is nothing nice about 'em they don't even look neat,
they all protrude from lumpy feet and bump the doors and beds
they're the first bit to meet anything - way out in front of heads.

Both rows start in the middle, then slope down to either side -
like the 'Pipes of Pan', but solid, what a blessing not as wide,
whatever nationality or creed, these things are God's creations
just little chunks of bone and flesh, all topped with hard crustaceans.

Now babies' toes are different, all soft and pink and chubby
they really are most loveable, although sometimes they're 'grubby',
but as we chase on through the years, these baby chipolatas
grow more each day in every way, to look like plum tomatoes.

But 'fingers' sticking out on hands, now that's another story
slender, supple, pink and soft with nails to top their glory,
we train them to do what we want, in fact most anything
from cooking, writing, zipping zips and even knotting string.

You can 'hold hands' but not 'hold feet' it simply can't be done
play 'footsie' if you want to - but that's not half the fun,
one thumb, four fingers and a palm all make a caring hand
but toes that decorate our feet, still fail to make them grand.

We have arms and legs and hips, and teeth that last for years
a nose to rest our glasses on and clip behind the ears.
All bits we own have uses, with care they'll last forever
toes just stop us falling over - though not pretty - that is clever.

Jim Pritchard

PARSLEY

Parsley is a humble herb.

And yet it has had its fill of calumny:
they call it the Devil's herb,
bringer of secret evil into the kitchen garden.
You are advised (we are advised)
to sow it on a holy day
so that the Devil would not snatch the seeds away -
and fly across darkening skies with his claws full of seeds
seeding the Earth below with a green growing contagion
bombing the Earth below with seeds of fire -
but saints would preserve it.

The difference in varieties is a modest difference:
French parsley has little flat leaves,
subtle distinction, like two heads of mousy hair,
one straight, and one curly.

No one says
'I think I'll have parsley for dinner tonight.
I will invite my lover to feast on parsley.'
Parsley only enhances other dishes:
broad beans, fillets of fish, a bowl of salad.
It does not head the menu.
It just gets along.

Put parsley on the flag of United Nations!
Make parsley the NATO banner, for God's sake:
not ignorant of evil, not unaccused
but gentle, mild, and familiar in many lands,
it would work well with garlic, blend in with ginger,
never confuse the workaday world with a film set,
would not discriminate or do injustice.
And people would plant peace, maybe. On holy days.

Eve Kimber

LINGER LONGER!

Long hot summers where friends met
Making daisy chains
On Girton Rec'

Cricket, football yes and more
Swings and roundabouts
Who's keeping score?

Courting couples in later years
Fun and games
Laughter - (and tears!)

A crafty smoke behind a tree
'Youth Club tonight!'
Oh! Did our neighbour see?

'I think she did'
'Will she tell Mum?'
Well too late I am undone

Looking back with some regret
I should have stayed a bit longer
On Girton Rec'!

Tricia Layton

Moods

Whenever I feel miserable, I try to think of things,
that make me laugh or have a bath, or put my hair in pins.
Another good idea I find, is make a cup of tea.
I don't know anyone who drinks as many cups as me.
If one can find a friend to chat with, that's a good idea,
yet, men when feeling miserable they have a glass of beer.

It's true one should indulge oneself if misery is the cause.
I like to have a chocolate bar, but then I stop and pause.
I am a chocoholic and one piece is not enough,
when I eat the whole of it, that makes me in a huff.
So, I guess I will be miserable oh heavens! I can see
I'll have to change my mood again and stay a happy me.

Molly Phasey

PISCES

Pisceans are the dreamers,
With vision, to put things right.
Revelling in discussion
'Seeing' words, as stronger than - might!

Loving, loyal, somewhat poetical,
They can outsmart, the best intellectual!
Very deep thinking and knowledgeable,
Analysing, tho' not judging, one and all!

A humour and charm, that wins your heart,
Even tempered, easy to love.
The Pisces nature, is friendly and kind,
A 'would be' hawk, who is really, a dove!

Their home, is their castle, yet with no need,
For the material things, they've no vanity to feed,
Aesthetic beauty, more their taste,
Their lives, are never lived in haste!

Independence, is important to them,
Honour, honesty, a way of their living,
There is an ethereal quality too,
A romance, to all of their - giving.

E M Eagle

BROCKHILL PARK - HYSTERICS IN THE HAIL

If you went for a walk, took some time for a talk
Packed a smart suitcase, filled with food for the place

If you got up at dawn, to make food for the morn
If you baked a breakfast quiche, made kebabs of fruit and peach

If you packed a pecan tart, brought cream to go on top
If the sun was shining happily, you walked as far as you could see

If your friends had come with you to share the beautiful view
Would you be content?

If the sky turned grey and hostile, and raindrops began to pile
Would you smile?
If the raindrops turned huge, then became a deluge
Would you giggle?
If the deluge became hail, in the middle of this gale
Would you laugh uncontrollably?

We would!

Carey Sellwood

THE THREE GHOSTLY MINERS

Hunched up in a corner, a miner sat and prayed
'Dear God, please send a rescue team,' his nerves were shot and frayed
'We're running out of oxygen, the roof it might cave in.
I'm sorry my life's been so bad and sorry I have sinned.
Just help the men with families, whose lives their wives depend,
It's getting hard to breathe down here, I fear it's near the end.
Our lamps are getting dimmer, our hearts are filled with fear.'
Whilst one voice said The Lord's Prayer, another shed a tear.
The mineshaft filled with water, the miners they all died,
Mothers mourned their young sons, the wives in black shawls cried,
I've heard a tale that on the eve, the miners all return
Back to the place where they all died, their lamps so brightly burn.
There was a rumble down below, explosions filled the air
Nine men were trapped in coal and dirt, their wives full of despair
Then all at once three men appeared, around them glowed a light,
They led the men to safety on that cold winter's night
And as they turned to thank them, they saw them disappear
Back down into the mineshaft, the miners shook with fear.
It was the ghostly miners who came to save the day
Then all at once the nine men dropped on their knees and prayed,
'Thank God you sent your angels with lamps that burned so bright
To guide us back to safety on that horrendous night.'

P Bradley

COULDN'T CARE LESS

There is always great sadness in dying,
Leaving relatives grieving for you,
But how many women are crying,
Over deaths that were not even due?
Think of all the young soldiers in battle,
To be fearful would only bring shame,
They're supposed to be mindless, like cattle,
Though engaged in a terminal game.
There are some with delusions of grandeur,
The remainder are quaking with dread,
They can run and then face the dishonour,
Or be honoured among the brave dead,
Just how many young men are unwilling,
To go to their end in this way,
Who abhor the idea of killing,
But they're just too damned frightened to say?
They're engaging in legalised murder,
They've to kill, or to perish instead,
And the leaders, who issue the orders?
They couldn't care less for the dead.

Matthew L Burns

SAND MARTINS

Some birds don't mind, how cold it is
All year they want to stay
Others find it much too cold
And decide to fly away.
Some fly down to Africa
Where it's warm and easy to feed
I don't know why they go that far
When they have to come back to breed.
They arrive here in April
So tired and without a rest
They dig out holes in the sand
And then start to make a nest.
These little birds are martins
They dart about all day
When they are not busy feeding
They sit on eggs that they lay.
The newborn babies sit and wait
In holes just showing their head
Those noisy little devils
Just waiting to be fed.
They are not a very big bird
So delicate and light
They are a sort of chocolate colour
With a little bit of white.
Then some time in September
It's time to fly away
Now the weather's changing
It's too cold for them to stay.

Barry G Randall

THE DULL LIFE

'What dreary lives we live,' the woman said.
'It's hardly worth getting out of bed
And it seems the time is slipping past
When every day is like the last
Without a chance to have some fun
When the dull day's work is done
I'm right fed up, I do declare
No sign of excitement anywhere
Just the same old boring dismal day
Why can't the sun come out to stay?
I wish the world could all be changed
And more excitement be arranged!'

Her companion laughed as a fire engine fast
Went clanging madly as it rushed past
Almost colliding with a big red bus
And all the passengers made a fuss.
They hardly heard the ambulance bell
Racing to save a poor man who fell
From off a ladder in the square
Whilst trying to rob the jewellers there.
The Daily News headline read 'The Sun
Is Playing Havoc With The Skin Of Everyone'.
They turned the corner and went indoors,
And soon a cup of tea she pours
'Ah! You can't beat a cup of tea,' she said.
'It keeps you going until you're dead!'

Len Corner

MOST OF ALL

I love to walk in sunshine,
down a country path,
or lie out in the garden,
or wallow in the bath.

To swim out in the ocean,
to sit outside the pub,
and have a glass of ale,
with some old friends that I love.

To take the dogs out walking,
high upon the moors,
or sit and paint in oils,
the beautiful outdoors.

To go and see a movie,
or go out and have a meal,
all these things I've mentioned,
to me they do appeal.

To go out with the children,
and play with their football,
but sitting home with you,
is what I love most of all.

Jeffrey Kelly

SPREAD A LITTLE SUNSHINE

All you need is the 'sun in the morning
And the moon at night,'
A little child's smile
Will put wrongs to right.

To feel good you just need the simplest things
Like a kiss, and a hug, each day,
A helping hand to those in need
To help them on their way.

Feeding crumbs to little birds
As they visit me every day,
Shows an act of kindness
Goes a long, long way.

I feel good myself being free from pain,
Just to be alive isn't profit, it's gain.
Most of all, like flowers in bud,
Even that, should make you all feel good.

Vera Ewers

ON COLOURED WINGS

Look at the beautiful butterflies
Out there, on the buddleia bush.
Flying here, and flying there
Always in a rush.

Golden Admiral, blue and white,
'Oh look at that one there
Dark brown, with bright pink markings,
It must be very rare.'

Along the fence comes a grey striped cat
And crouches as it waits
To catch a lovely butterfly
As it lands upon the gate.

They live on the food of the buddleia bush,
On its nectar they descend.
Butterflies live not very long
From pupa to the end.

They also rest on the lavender bush
Amongst the purple scented flowers.
As the bees come to gather their nectar
They flit, between the bowers.

No artist can paint their beautiful colours,
Reds, pinks, browns and gold.
No tapestry can show them at their best
Even when it is old.

Don't put them in a cold glass case
Where they will lie alone and forgot.
Let them fly into the sky,
Until they become just a dot.

Who gave them all these delicate hues
On tiny, fragile wings?
Our God designed them for this world
To beautify all things.

Joan Smith

DOWN ON THE FARM

We got us a 'point of lay' pullet,
Whose eggs shot out like a bullet.
Some of them oval, some of them round:
Some missed the target and were never found.

So we traded her in and got us a pig.
She slept by the fire, until she got big.
Then she wallowed in mud in her little sty
What heaven, what bliss, then she did die.

So off we went and bought us a sheep,
She would not stop bleating, we got no sleep.
We got her a ram, just to keep her quiet,
Baby lambs everywhere, causing a riot!

So we traded them all in and got us a goat.
The goat was long-haired, what a coat.
The goat ate everything, including us.
. . . !

Maggy Copeland

I Do It To Music Occasionally
(Reflections on Sir Michael Tippett's Oratorio)

I do it to music occasionally,
    Or possibly music does it to me.
Music wells up on its opulent swells.
    Torrents break forth like freshets down spring fells.

Ah crahd uh rivuh, Ah donnoh wah.
    Mebbeh wehn laugh's all cracked an drah:
Lack peynt danna front of an ol hass wall,
    Annah reynpahp's chocked up wid dirt an all;
Tear ducts damn-up an music sloos a dose
    Of overdoo lachrymose fluids, Ah suppose.

Owen Watson

REPORT CARD

The report cards are coming!
The report cards are coming!
Hear the electricity humming

Suspense saturated classroom air
Attention rigid back neck hair
Muscles tight from head to toes
Perspiration buds and flows

Double marching mind wheels turn
Stomach curdles in the churn
Gnawing nerves can't stand at ease
See the sight of knocking knees

The report cards are here!
The report cards are here!
Smell and taste the fear

Quickly quiet connects around
Receive reports with no earth sound
Some shocking shivers and joule jolts
From tension of 10,000 volts

Timidly turning performance pages
Drilling to detail takes up ages
Positive, negative, neutral phrases
But overall salutes and praises

The report card is good!
The report card is good!
Feel the sense of relief . . .

Andrew Younger

JOURNEY AFLOAT

Starting the day from Thorpe St Andrew,
As we board the boat, all checks are made.
We unpack our cases, and have a cup of tea.
Three children are present, one dog in tow.
We fasten our life jackets,
As we say off we go.

The river is smooth and the trees so still,
We take a long deep sigh, as we release our burden
From day to day living.
At 5mph and checking our speed, watching the landscape,
As we potter along.
Examine our maps for mooring up spaces,
As we moor up the boat and have dinner afloat.

The ropes tied up tight,
And the mud weight on front.
As we sit on board our boat,
Studying our maps for the day.

An hour of relaxing, as we set off for the day,
We unknot our ropes, as we set on our way.
The windmills and abbey ruins on the journey,
We take in the scenery, as we voyage along.

The views are amazing, and very pleasing,
To find a mooring spot, tie up for the night.
The day is complete, as we reflect on the
Memories the day has left us with.

Sharon Christian

MAGIC SPOT

I love this spot
When the weather's hot,
With the sun so high
In a deep blue sky.

I love this hill
When I've had my fill
Of worry and care,
And need fresh air.

I love this stone
As I sit on my own
Surveying the view
Vibrant and true.

I love this seat,
It's such a treat
To sit and dream
By this peaceful scene.

I love being here
In this spot so dear.
It will always be
The place for me.

S J Dodwell

END IN SIGHT

Already you have travelled too far.
Which road to take? You hesitate -
If you look up and glimpse a star
you'll know that you've left it too late . . .
If that should prove so, why persist?
Rolling towards you, see the mist.

The mountain looming to one side
assumes the shape of crouching beast.
Your footsteps quicken to a stride.
- A wind comes screaming from the east -
- but its force and din disappear -
- left all the brooding landscape here.

The mist in front takes ghostly form
and is all you have to follow.
Far rather would you dare a storm
then a greyness that can swallow
the sky above and land around.
How can what you seek now be found?

The mist swallows into itself
all substance and solidity,
undermines awareness, health -
- encroaches upon sanity.
The mountain still a hidden threat . . .
What's left behind cause for regret.

Swift as it came, mist rolls away
enough light left to find the bay.

C M Creedon

WALKING IN THE DARK

We go for a walk
And as dogs cannot talk
I can't ask where we are going,
So there is no way of knowing.
It's really only you who know
I cannot see the way to go.
Then suddenly I feel alone
As I am often these days prone,
However, using my nose to smell
I can quite easily tell
Just where you now are,
And it's really not very far,
So I'll catch up OK
'Well done, Old Chap,' you'll say.
Still I do wish I could see,
This isn't like the old me.
But at least I do have you
Always guiding me through.

Joan Chapman

A Cry From The Heart

They say flowers are coloured,
Skies sometimes are blue
But when you are blind
Is that really true?
How do you know? Where do you go?

A bird when in flight
May be large or quite small,
Is it there now at all?
I can't tell - oh what hell.

When you pick up a book
Folk say, 'Look!' but no good.
Instructions on how to cook,
'Look' - how I wish that I could
I can't see, what's there for me.

I can feel, touch and smell
I am strong, young and well
But the colours I can't tell.
What is yellow? What is blue?
Oh my goodness, if only I knew!
What is red? What is pink?
It puzzles me and I can't think.
It goes round in my head, till I'm near dead.

Doctors are now trying to cope
With blindness to give hope.
Just give us light where there is dark
To see a bird, perhaps a lark.
Without hope we nearly choke
Dear Lord just give us hope.

Jacqueline Bartlett

WHISPERS

Whispers in the classroom fill me with dread,
As I'm sure someone was once alive here and now they are dead.
I clean in the mornings, on my own,
So why do I feel, that I'm not alone?
With the hoovering done and just the mopping to go,
I hurry to finish as I don't want to be slow.
I've worked here two years now, no one else would stay long
And when I'm feeling nervous I burst into song.
School holidays are the worst,
As my body trembles as if it were cursed.
Eight hours I've got to clean in one day,
The school scares me so, as I long to go home far away
From my tortured mind that plays tricks on me
Oh why
Isn't there another school cleaner please?
I've begged my boss for another to help
But she just says, 'Two cleaners are enough!'

J M Stoles

YES, IT'S GOOD

It's good to write,
It's good to hear,
It's good to send a word of cheer.

It's good to exchange,
It's good to express,
It's good to expand on traumas and stress.

It's good to care,
It's good to share,
It's good to send happiness everywhere.

It's good to live,
It's good to know,
It's good to feel friendship steadily grow.

It's good to laugh,
It's good to love,
It's good to bring peace like a dove.

It's good to receive,
It's good to be aware,
It's good to live knowing others have time to spare.

It's good to send
A card with a greeting,
Bringing memories of a special meeting.

Time quickly passes, life is so fleeting,
Yes, it's so good to write your thoughts and greeting.

Stella Bush-Payne

AUNTIE ETHEL'S GHOST

When Auntie Ethel comes to stay
you're not allowed to go and play.
You have to talk about the war
cos Auntie Ethel is a bore!

When Auntie's here you can't eat sweets -
cos Auntie Ethel steals your treats.
She claims they make your teeth a sight,
but hers are false so *she's* alright!

When Auntie Ethel came to stay,
it was a lovely summer's day.
But when she said that she should go -
the sky outside had turned to snow!

So next time Auntie baked a flan,
Dad came up with a cunning plan
and when she came to stay once more
Dad groaned and screamed behind the door!

We let her in, she looked quite pale
we hung her coat upon a nail.
We sat her down, we brought her toast
and told her all about our ghost!

At first, she thought it was a game,
until this voice called out her name!
(It was our dad under the stairs -
enough to give poor Aunt nightmares!)

He rattled my bicycle chain
and groaned like he had gone insane!
Her tea went flying in the air,
while toast and jam went everywhere!

And since that day, she's not been round,
and ghostly noises? Not a sound!
She hasn't phoned or left a note -
or even come to fetch her coat!

Andrew Detheridge

HASTINGS

How many times have I been to Hastings?
How many times will I go again?
The smell of nets and cockles just haunts me
And tales from the old fishermen.
From little quaint pubs whose walls tell a story
Of hardship and perils at sea.
To modern hotels with shiny new bells
And maids serving afternoon tea.
How many times have I been to Hastings?
How many times, I don't know.
I know it is many, so save every penny
And join me the next time I go.

John Wayre

LIFE NEAR THE STREAM

The lovely little stream runs from the waterfall
Past the big hole below,
Under the tree growing out from the bank and up
But not stopping the flow.

Ripples over the stones so smooth, onto the pool
Where fish and eels do lie.
The kingfisher's nest, full of bones is in the bank
And to the pool he'll fly.

On over the stepping stones, and under the bridge
Past the wood and flowers.
Round the corner, where the voles live, then turn again
This goes on for hours.

Nothing so lovely as this stream, onto the bridge
A brick one at this time
With trees growing each side, it's a picture to see
And all is in its prime.

It's like Heaven on Earth, as the dragonflies dart
And the kingfishers flash
The beautiful blue, then he comes to his rest
To feed babies with panache.

Edith Buckeridge

WHISPERING SHADOWS

I lurk in the shadows and creep in the night.
Invisible to eye, I'm out of sight.

I am the darkness that surrounds you in bed,
And the visions of nightmares that appear in your head.

I am the creaks and the bumps that you hear,
And the hairs on your neck that stand up with fear.

I am the wind as it howls at your door,
And the heavy rain that starts to pour.

I am the mist and the clouded fog,
And the echoing barks of a lonely dog.

I fill your head with anger and hate.
You are blind but can see what I create.

What I am is not clear to see,
But I can change fate, I'm a mystery.

D J Abbott

DAY TRIPS

As I wander this lonely shore,
Thoughts and memories do haunt me more.
I feel a stirring in my heart, and then the tears begin to start,
And these will go on for a while
But parts of my memory will make me smile.
Familiar thoughts then enter my mind,
I hear the laughter of every child.
Their screams of delight as they jump into the sea,
What wonderful days they used to be.
We stroll on the prom,
Perhaps buy a little gift for family and friends.
We wish these days would never end,
But they do, and it's time to go home.
And over the years the children grow up,
And soon have a life of their own.
Then my memory grows dim and I'm back on the shore,
I look at the beach and walk some more.
The sand stretching out,
Never ending it seems,
And the rocks rising high, almost touching the sky.
The melancholy cry of the gulls as they come in to land.
Not another sound to be heard,
Just the breaking of waves on the sand.
This place is deserted this time of the year,
All the shops boarded up and just standing bare.
But memories my darling can still make me smile,
If I just sit down and dream for a while.

Tom Usher

DIY

Patrick Corner was not a man
It was a self assembly kit,
A computer desk of many parts
Each piece exactly made to fit.

All sorts of bits to join together
Clear instructions noted on 20 pages,
Patience would be an asset here
Or this project may take me ages.

I opened the box and stood aghast
At the sight before my eyes,
Thought two hours would be enough
I was in for a big surprise.

I set to work without worry
On hands and knees, tools nearby,
Fitting each section step by step
I've done this before this DIY.

I laboured on slow but sure
Pleased with my good workmanship,
Two sides built in record time
Mustn't let my concentration slip.

Some hours later it was almost done
Although larger than I anticipated,
However it was looking very chic
A computer desk to be appreciated.

The unit was positioned with due care
Then I installed all the hi-tech stuff,
Seven hours it had only taken me
By then I surely had had enough.

My knees and back were aching
But happy now the jigsaw was complete,
Beech-coloured veneer, a lovely choice
Now all I needed was a comfortable seat.

George S Johnstone

WISHING YOU SAFE

I'd climb the highest mountain
and swim the deepest sea.
If only things were
as they used to be.

But, you are a soldier
and must fight a war,
fight for man's freedom
and peace for evermore.

As you face the danger,
be assured of my love.
Every day a prayer for you
wings up to Heaven above.

I pray that God will,
keep you safe from harm
and send you very soon
into my waiting arms.

Julie Brown

THE POOR POTATO

Has anyone thought of the potato
Sometimes we call it the spud
We dig up the ground and bury it
In all the sticky mud.

The potato gets a raw deal
We even take off its peel
We chop it in two to put in a stew
Boil it and mash it too.

We roast it and sometimes bake
All our dinners to make
We also cut out its eyes to make our pies
And dehydrate it to make it a fake.

We slice it in bits to make our chips
We stab it and pierce it too
Also chop it and crisp it, mix with butter and whisk it.
What a how do you do!

So next time you eat potato
And it's steaming all hot and nice
Ask yourself whether it would rather
Be snuggled in a bed of ice.

Violetta Jean Ferguson

NO QUIET PLACE

There is no secret place
From others to be aside.
Where of others there is no trace
To be removed and hide.
It seems a plaintiff hope
For others with a similar dream strive
A problem in common we cope
To solve the problem we are ill-blessed.
Where solace used to be found
Though with reservations I express
Others are likely to be bound
As if by profligate nature sown
But if their actions I condemn
And in gesture their actions disown
I remember I am but a clone of them.

Brian Norman

FINDON

In the hollow of the Downs lies Findon
Where sheep roam free and shepherds call
And sheepdogs round them one and all
Where the Cissbury Ring towers high above
There suitors walk and fall in love
Then over on the skyline's hue
The Chantonbury Ring's in view
A timeless spot, a haunting place
Where life is calm and slow of pace
Here the Saxon tilled and made his mark
The Sussex Downs were his park
Then the Norman's conquering hand
Held the Saxon to his bonded land
Forced him to toil his earthly sod
And bow to Norman rule and god
Land was taxed and the English shook
When William filled his Domesday Book
With records of their wealth and dues
To the Normans, pride, they had to lose
But there deep beneath the earth
The Saxon's pride, the Saxon's birth
Live on in the hollow of the Downs and Findon.

G Carpenter

A Case Of Conflict

Oh forgive, forget, politicians proclaim
To who all fought their great war game!
But try as we will in night hours alone -
Those aching bones injuries, with thoughts to atone!

In heated nightmares we live them again
Amidst flying shells, missiles and our pain
Off goes the pillar, flung now the arms -
Helping drown sailors, with their lucky charms!

Squeals from injured sailors, howl in despair
As each ship flounders - out over there -
Old friends struggle in water, sharks there I see
Hardly a hope of a rescue from any of we!

Yelling aloud - in the night air, all despair
These enemy b******s not a heart to care,
Machine gunning in water, to finish them, shoot,
Germans with bloodlust, know what to hoot!

Forgive them Father our politics ask too
That place men in conflict like me and you
Then ask us to forgive - settle and be
Friends for our futures - how can it be?

Conflict's the cause by - politics I see!
Make them head battles - answer as we!
For enemies' actions - injured and lost!
They seem not to count - in spite of the cost!

Geoffrey Wilyman

THE WAVE

Here
Comes the crashing wave
I really must be brave.

Watery
Forces claw at my legs
Pulling me down and back.

Slipping
Away from the safe shore
To the frightening pebble maelstrom.

Breathe
Gasp. I'm rolled about
Which way is up? Which way is down?

Panic
I can't breathe but I see a light
Air, sun, safety, I'm alive! I cannot wait
To try another wave.

S Woodland

GALLOPING ON THE MOOR

A time I often do recall
Is riding on the Moor
With wind so strong and showers of rain
Makes your face quite cold and sore.

The reins now difficult to hold
They slip out of your hand
Galloping up the grass so fast
On huge expanse of land.

The pace is so exhilarating
And power of mighty steed
I can't go nearly fast enough
As I gather up more speed.

The visibility now quite poor
I hear thundering hooves behind
Then my horse really takes hold
And flat out, it pounds the ground.

I can't think of more enjoyment
Or a better place to be
Than to ride upon the Moor
What pleasure it gives me.

C Armstrong

LIFE'S STORY

Our life is a book full of stories,
The half of which hasn't been told.
We can read them to children and grown-ups
But not ourselves till we're old.

There are stories for children and parents.
Of joy and of sorrow untold.
Of sheep that have strayed on the mountain,
And the Shepherd brought back to the fold.

Many chapters there be in life's story,
Birth and death and sorrows untold.
The suffering and life long devotion,
In troubles and sickness and woe.

But a chapter of Blessings unnumbered,
Received from our Father on High.
For He loveth His children immensely,
And giveth them treasures so right.

We're writing sad stories or glad ones,
Each day indelibly we write.
For good or bad our influence,
On those we meet day or night.

Make sure your story blesses -
The one who picks up and reads,
Its many pages and chapters
For you cannot turn back or recede.

R Baker

THE DENTIST

Off to the dentist for a three-monthly check up
Lie back, open wide your gob
My heart starts to throb

The dentist he doth prod and poke
I assure you this is no joke
Can he find a cavity?
A little bit of sensitivity

Occlusal, distal, mesial, where will this hole be?
Relax, he cannot find
So now I shall eat meals that are tooth-kind.

Christine M Wicks

MOTCOMBE PARK

Walking past the ducks
As they splash and tuck
Their tails in
Behind the Lamb Inn
Towards the roses
Which soon form posies
Past where Dad's ashes are
The pond reflects his vibrant star
Where he resides peacefully
I watch his steps faithfully
Children's voices resonate
Across the grass that decorates
The bowling green so smooth
Discarded feathers to remove
In the evening time
Of weather, flint and lime
The Church Tower glows
And the bell sounds with hammer blows
Motcombe Park gates shut
Paint and rust near the hut
Peace reigns supreme for now
As the moon makes a solemn vow.

Tim Sharman

Tears

My tears fall soft upon my face
They tumble down without a trace

I am crying

My sorrow it is cold and aching
It rests upon a heart that's breaking

I am crying

My face it wears a sunny smile
My eyes are cloaked with clever guile

I am crying

The day is drawing to a close
Night-time has come and no one knows

I am crying

S M Ilsley

WATCH THE TV

I just watch the TV
Sitting by the fire every night
With my family using the other rooms
It is a sight so nice.

I just watch the TV
Until it is time for my bed
Whereupon I climb the stairs
Nodding my weary head.

I just watch the TV
Because nobody speaks at all
Not even my best friends
Think to give me a call.

Keith L Powell

POETRY

Write a bit of poetry
I wonder on what theme?
What will the judges want of me,
to give pleasure as they read?

I have already sent to them
a poem of mine to read
but never did they say to me -
thank you - or yes indeed.

I wonder will I try again
and see what I can do
to try and win a special prize
for my poetry that is me.

B Spinks

FACES IN THE CROWD

Take a walk down a busy street
Look at all the people you meet
Then look at their walk and grace
Finally take a good look at the face.

One could look like Gene Kelly
Just as he looked on the telly
You can imagine him doing a dance
Before you turn away your glance.

Then there is a little girl
With Shirley Temple curls
You expect her to break into song
Before she moves gaily along.

Next who do we meet
As we move down the street?
Is that Coronation Jack I see
Coming right up to me?

He is asking me the way
What do I really say -
Are you Jack? Or tell him the way
Before he moves quickly on his way?

So you could create your own cast
From the people that you pass
With all these different lookalikes
I guess that is what I would like.

Jean Bradbury

SUMMER CAMP IN AMERICA

What a lovely summer to remember!
From June through to the end of September,
Camp Timber Ridge in West Virginia,
Nine weeks camp, five weeks round America.

Camping in cabins, work in the laundry,
Meals in the dining hall. Saturday's free,
Children playing, swim in the swimming pool,
Sports and activities for Summer School

Beautiful views of Shenandoah Mountains,
Trips to Winchester shopping and fountains,
Canoes on the River Cacopan,
Horse riding, barbecues, art and suntan.

After the camp, a month on Amtrak train,
To see American country again.

S M Robertson

THE PAINTBRUSH

As I looked about me, swaying in the breeze,
I saw the loggers coming through the trees.
I was shortly to be felled and sent to the sawmill,
Where they would decide what to make of me.

Now I'm Ashley, the paintbrush, born of an ash tree,
I was nearly made into a matchstick.
What a future! One puff and you're gone!
But as a paintbrush now, my soul could benefit.

I was put on display in an art shop
And a Miss Penelope from Dundee bought me.
She put me in a jam jar with another paintbrush
Whose name I learnt was Pinette of the Pinetree.

We took turn and turn about painting on the canvas,
And I soon realised it was evolving into a love affair,
Pinette with dainty sweeping strokes like a fanfare,
But, one morning when I woke up, she wasn't there.

Next day I heard a rumour, she's gone to paint the queen,
My Pinette, to paint Her Royal Highness Christine.
What an honour! But oh how I miss her.
Come back to me, wind of the pinetree.

As I was head down in the turps, I couldn't see where,
But surely they would take me too, we're a pair.
I dried my bristles, which gleamed from the turps
And put a bow tie on my fresh shirt.

At length, Pinette returned, more beautiful than ever,
And I proposed to her with an Edwardian bow.
She accepted and Miss Penelope, to the gardens of Kew
Sent us, there to receive an everlasting accolade of our prowess.

Rosemary Smith

AH VANITY!

We like your style,
Or so they say,
You should go on a mile
If only you pay,
A little to us
Before we bring out a book,
So all the fine people
Can come have a look.

And you thought it was free,
With a big fat fee,
What riddlemaree.
And who will then buy
This pie-in-the-sky?
But don't give up hope,
Though it's game,
Rope-a-dope.

Alistair McLean

MODERN TIMES

Why the popularity of pop-art, what is the objective or aim?
Common objects become popular and rare objects defamed.
The beautiful, talented person or star is relentlessly targeted and chased,
By camera or crowd and their image multiplied and debased.

Everyday objects are portrayed, studied for deep inner meaning.
While unique, complex works of art left unnoticed or demeaned.
The commonplace becomes trendy and rare, unique, object unprotected.
That which should be respected, is wantonly ignored or neglected.

People who are good and beautiful are scrutinised openly for flaw.
While the bad, ugly and evil are left alone to live unnoticed by law.
Minor themes become major and great deal made of little things.
Art that took time, patience, talent and skill is often demoted.
While random, ugly and shapeless art is shamelessly promoted.

Celebrity good deeds are overlooked, their weakness accentuated.
Sins appear greater than good and scandal is obsessively investigated,
To fill public appetite for news of celebrities regardless of pain.
Laws should protect privacy of individual - regardless of station.
For pain and injustice to one person affects all people in the nation!
The modern trend, is turn upside down, bad is good, wrong - right
All art and ideals are viewed in this new, ugly, perverted light!

Patricia McQueen

RISE AND SHINE

Morning sun your tender rays
Are shining down on me
While I lie upon my bed
Awakening from a dream

My head's a haze my eyes are soaked
The colours in my room
Are swelling up inside my mind
Destroying darkened gloom

The golden thrush he sings his song
While catching early worms
The melody comes floating through my brain
And leaves a thought inside my mind
Of soothing velvet rain

To rise and dress and head for work
Means nothing to me now
For I have felt the soothing touch
Of nature on my brow

Alan Johnson

HERE COMES THE SUN

As you open your bedroom window,
The warm air glides in on an early morning breeze.

As you walk out of your front door,
You feel the warmth of the summer air.

As you drive along the country roads,
You are woken to wonderful summer sights.

As you arrive home at night,
You can still see the young children
Laughing and running over the open fields.

Jessie Coffey (13)

TIME

Time is something which goes quickly every day
Most of us realise this anyway
Life seems to go so very quick
Even if you're healthy or even sick

We start our childhood with much joy
If you are a girl or a boy
But very soon we enter our teens
And lots of us start wearing jeans

We start courting soon anyway
And most of us end up marrying, one day
Then our children start to arrive
There can be as many as four or five

When we are middle aged soon anyway
And our children are growing up every day
We look forward to our grandchildren
Which will come one day
They give us lots of love anyway
Even if we feel older anyway.

Yes, time goes at a pace all the time
And now we are grandparents and the children we love
They really must be sent by God above
We get from them lots of joy and pleasure
And we love to play with them at our leisure.

When we are really old one day
Too old to do much anyway
We wonder how our life has gone so quickly
The children try to help us all they can
And make us think when life began

So we must realise time has passed
And we are really old at last
We must thank God for the good life we have had
Even if sometimes things seem a bit bad

And now we are really old at last
And we love to think about our past
Now we must realise our days are going fast
And soon we will be going to God at last.

Kay Taylor

CALL OF DEVON

The call of the lonely moorland
The grey of the stormy sky
The heather lined lanes of Devon
Remind me of days gone by

The Dart at its best is running
Fast, clean and free
And hope ever eternal
Reaches out to me

The granite grey and sombre
Stands steadfast and true
It beckons me onward
To where the river runs blue

The sight of this wild moorland
Pulls the strings of my heart
And walking the vast open spaces
I know I will never depart

Margaret Gurney

WAITING FOR YOU

In morning mist and new fallen dew,
Faint hints of dawn touch a far horizon;
An early blackbird pours out a song
Of such beauty, to this earth it does not belong,
The world is at peace, awaiting the day.
Sheltered by oak, and ancient yew,
I wait here alone, waiting for you.

Through midday heat and the sun at its height,
Weary and bent by the burdens of life
Carried on shoulders too old to care,
Eyes have grown dim, whitening hair.
An end to toil, a blessed relief
As life enters twilight, welcomes the night.
So many years, waiting for you.

In eventide calm, hushed is the day;
Its labours are spent, earth is at rest.
In the deep of the darkness, the spirit finds peace
In stillness and silence, a dear-bought release.
Ghostly thoughts of what might have been,
Dreams that were broken on life's winding way.
My day is ended, waiting for you.

M Marshall

FALSE APRIL

Love roared in like a hurricane
To swiftly capture heart and mind
And caution's pleas were all in vain
To deafened ears and eyes made blind.

Love swept in like the ocean's tide
That would not pause but surging free,
Cast all reckoning aside.
So it was when love found me.

I sailed that glorious tide with you.
Bright April's sunshine filled our days.
All life, with mine, began anew
When you taught me love's wild sweet ways.

But journeys end; the year moves on.
Now sighing shallows soothe the shore
And weeping clouds know love has gone.
My lonely heart will sing no more.

Pat Saunders

JUBILEE

We all came to London
Just to see
Our queen celebrate
Her jubilee.
The crowds they gathered
From far and wide,
In Birmingham, Slough
And Humberside.
All over the country
Young and old
Not stopped by anything
Rain or cold.
We all came together
Our God to praise
For 50 years
Of golden days.

Mary Crowhurst

UNTITLED

Will spring come back next year
And when it does, will I be here?
To see the yellow flowers
That always welcome spring,
To see the meadow clear of snow
To see the colours that now
Transform meadow grass to many hues.
Will I be here?
When spring returns next year
To hear songbirds welcoming
The return of spring.
Will I be here?
I've had my share
Of spring's delights I know,
So when I lie at rest
As dust upon that meadow green,
Will I be kissed by spring's soft wind
That played with my love's soft hair?
As we laid upon that meadow green.

Arthur J Pullen

EATING COMPANION

Chocolates, cakes,
All piling up
Waiting for someone
To gobble them up

Eating for comfort
When feeling lost and alone

Look in the cupboard,
Look in the fridge,
What shall I have
To end up like a pig?

Fatter and fatter
I'm getting to be
If only there was someone
Who could be here with me

Joanne Wilcock

THE WASHING

'Blow wind blow'
said the washing on the line
'We should be dry by now
just look at the time.'

The fluffy white towel
thought it was a laugh
'I should be in the bathroom
when Johnny has his bath.'

'Hurry, do hurry'
said the sheet for the bed
'He's got to have somewhere
to lay his sweet head.'

The shirt, sleeves a-flapping
cried out in dismay
'Please get a move on
I can't hang here all day.'

'Oh!' Cried the tablecloth
in some despair
'The dinner's on the table
and I'm not there!'

C Matthews

NEW FOUND CONFIDENCE

Protruding teeth like ugly fangs, my mouth I could not close,
I was teased unmercifully, which filled me full of woe,
Every time I tried to speak, my tongue strayed in the way
Those who stood beside me received a shot of spray.
The dentist said 'Don't worry, I'll fit you with a brace.'
It wasn't very long before I saw improvement to my face.
I'm grateful for her expertise, my life has changed for free
Now the 'ring of confidence', is surrounding me.

Doreen Kowalska

THE SHADOW

I came to this broken down old house,
The door was opened wide,
Curiosity got the better of me,
So I looked inside.
I called out 'Anyone here?'
As I stepped into the room.
No sign or sound of anyone,
A room of darkness and gloom.
So I ventured up the stairs,
No carpets on the floor.
I came to a bedroom
Quiet, no sound at all.
Wallpaper was hanging because of damp
From every single wall.
Then I became aware
Of a shadow by the fireplace
'Hello' I said 'how are you?'
But I could not see a face
Then the shadow went.
No idea where.
I told people in the village
'It's the truth I swear.'
'The house has been empty ten years,' they said.
'Since the old lady passed away.
You must have seen the ghost of old Mrs Brady
She visits the house every day.'

D Field

WISHFUL THINKING

I am paid to rule Great Britain
Take advice from all my mates
My mates are not always honest
I pay for their mistakes

I never lie or do anything wrong
Have you not seen my wings?
One day I will be president
Then I can do my own thing

I will make the world a better place
Have police in every street
Narrow the gap between rich and poor
Poverty will be no more

I will jail the men who dare to defy me
Shut the mouths of slandering tongues
I will hang the rapist and murderers
Cut off the hands of thieves

I promise not to spend too much money
Only one plane, one ship and two cars
I will not make idle promises
I will act without much talk

If only you will give me one more chance
To prove how good I am
I will work my fingers to the bone
But I warn you, beware if you don't!

Hetty Foster

THE BEAN SHAPED TREE

He stood upon the grass verge,
And nature made its urge,
In full view of the press
His Highness was absurd.
He had a handy wee thing,
And childishly withdrew,
His penis, and there did a widdle,
It was in fullest view.

The cameras all clicked,
And the child in wonder grew,
Bewildered that his handy wee thing,
Could land all in a stew.
His father was astounded,
His mother angry too,
That he should widdle
In the park, with his wee
Handy thing in view.

The royal pee was fertile,
And there sprang up a tree,
So broad and tall and bean-shaped,
It was a joy to see.

The prince became His Majesty,
And then he did decree
That all royal princes,
Must widdle behind the tree,
Where absolutely no one,
Had the ability to see.

Jean Bald

ANCHOR BOOKS
SUBMISSIONS INVITED
SOMETHING FOR EVERYONE

ANCHOR BOOKS - Any subject, light-hearted clean fun, nothing unprintable please.

THE OPPOSITE SEX - Have your say on the opposite gender. Do they drive you mad or can we co-exist in harmony?

THE NATURAL WORLD - Are we destroying the world around us? What should we do to preserve the beauty and the future of our planet - you decide!

All poems no longer than 30 lines.
Always welcome! No fee!
Plus cash prizes to be won!

Mark your envelope (eg *The Natural World*)
And send to:
Anchor Books
Remus House, Coltsfoot Drive
Peterborough, PE2 9JX

**OVER £10,000 IN POETRY PRIZES
TO BE WON!**

Send an SAE for details on our New Year 2003 competition!